Yes, You CAN Get That JOB!

Joanne Meehl, M.S., IJCDC
aka *The Job Search Queen*

Copyright © 2009 by Joanne Meehl. All rights reserved.

No part of this book may be reproduced in any form or by any electronic or mechanical means, including information storage and retrieval systems, without permission in writing from the publisher.

Printed in the United States of America

ISBN 978-0-9818720-0-1

Library of Congress Control Number: 2009925125

For information about ordering this publication for your school, career center, or organization, please contact us. Discount pricing and customizing options are available upon request.

Satya House Publications, Inc.
Special Markets
P. O. Box 122
Hardwick, Massachusetts 01037
(413) 477-8743

orders@satyahouse.com
www.satyahouse.com/getthatjob.htm

Cover illustration by Jessie Katz

SATYA HOUSE PUBLICATIONS
Hardwick, Massachusetts

For today's students . . . tomorrow's employees.

Introduction

If you are reading this, you are probably among the majority who will not be getting a BMW for graduation, or going to work in your uncle's Fortune 100 corporation after spending the summer abroad. You might be feeling a bit of anticipatory anxiety tempered by excitement, similar to what you felt the month before freshman year began. However, the stakes are now a lot higher. Along with your newly acquired degree is a newly acquired debt load. You don't have to figure out what classes to take; you have to FIND A JOB — preferably one that doesn't involve flipping burgers, and preferably one that allows you to pay rent to people other than your parents.

Yes, You Can Get That Job! was created to help you successfully navigate the limbo between college and the "real world," especially in economically turbulent times. As I'm sure you know, there are many career guides in the bookstores and on-line, and also quite a few thesauri. Until now, however, there have been none that combine the best aspects of both, and none specifically written for college seniors and new alumni trying to land their first post-graduate job.

During this (and subsequent) job searches, your primary task is to communicate your value to a potential employer. Without the ability to communicate effectively at every stage in the process, you won't get the job you want. Although you might be highly qualified for the job you want, you still have to persuade several other people that they won't regret hiring you.

This book will teach you to use words and resources a little bit differently than you did as a student. It will teach you to "sell" yourself more effectively than your competitors, and you will definitely have plenty of those.

Job Search and Key Words
First, from the thesaurus side of the page, this book contains only words that are relevant to a job search, even beyond the resume. So, although you won't find eight synonyms for the word *snow,* you will find seventeen for *ability.*

You'll also notice that the words are not field-specific. They don't focus on business, chemistry or child psychology. Every field has its own lexicon and by now, you should know that collection of terms for your major even better than I do.

Company Secret
Here's something you might not know. Companies generate a list of key words for each of their job categories. Some of the words are related to particular skills and experiences required for a particular job. Others are related to the type of person who would best fill the job. Still others come from the company culture, which can frequently be found throughout their web site and other communications. All these key words are entered into a database that is accessed by a software program that screens resumes and searches for matches.

Databases Are King
Think of your resume as a small key word database. Your key word database must match the employer's large key word database in order to be "flagged" for an actual human being to read. Without such key words, your resume won't ever get looked at. Even when a company or organization has human screeners, key words are still important. They are what you use to make a connection between you and them. It's that connection that gets you noticed.

This book will help you bridge the connection between what you've accomplished in your own studies, internships, and jobs, and the mind of the decision-maker who's looking at your resume or the software that's screening it. Hiring managers take about 3-5 seconds to skim your resume before deciding if they want to read further. Make it as effective as you can so they read it, match you to the job, and then call you in for the interview.

Quotes from the Queen

No, we're not kidding. The tips you'll find in this book may not be as valuable as the Crown Jewels, but in the overall scheme of things, they will be much more practical. So chuckle now, but I guarantee you'll appreciate them when you accept your first job offer. You'll find:

- Tips about networking.
- Tips about the job search in general, and more specifically
- Suggestions for just about anything you can think of during the search.
- Occasional narrative about a particular word or phrase: its pros, cons, best usage, when to avoid it, etc.
- Support for the writing tasks of your job search,
- and help with various job search tools.

I have extensive experience in career choice counseling, career planning, and job search coaching. During their job search, I share the following statements with my clients:

- Some lucky employer out there is looking for you. You just have to find them . . . and that takes work.
- Do the work and use the tools that will work for you to get the job YOU want, because you are worth it!

These simple statements have great value. You might not recognize that now, but they're true. Having faith in yourself goes a long way towards achieving any goal, not just landing a good job. In today's volatile job market, this belief in your value gives you a competitive edge.

Your Ideas Can Help Next Year's Graduating Class

As you search for a job, you might come up with some word ideas or other tips that worked well for you. For future editions, send them to:

Joanne@TheResumeQueen.com

Good luck with the search and welcome to the "real world."

— Joanne Meehl

A

Ability
Aptitude, capability, capacity, command, competence, dexterity, expertise, faculty, intelligence, know-how, knowledge, power, proficiency, qualification, skill, strength, talent

Accelerate
Advance, build, drive, expedite, facilitate, forward, hasten, increase, move, progress, push, quicken, speed up

Accomplish(ed)
Verbs: Achieve, attain, carry through, carry out, complete, execute, finish, fulfill, gain, meet, produce, reach, realize, succeed

Adjectives: Able, adept, competent, experienced, proficient, qualified

Accurate
Careful, certain, conclusive, correct, definite, detailed, exact, factual, infallible, methodical, official, perfect, precise, specific

Achieve
Accomplish, acquire, actualize, attain, carry through, complete, conclude, earn, effect, execute, finish, fulfill, gain, hit, obtain, make, perform, produce, reach, realize

Acquire
Achieve, amass, assume, attain, earn, gain, incur, obtain, realize

Quotes From The Queen

Attitude: Whose attitude? Yours, and the person in the position to hire you.

Yours, upbeat and confident: "Here's what I can do for you." Not "I have a 3.75 GPA." Today, a high GPA is just not enough.

Theirs, 99% of the time: "I hope this is the person we hire! We have so much work piling up, and other managers are on my case to get it done. Please let this one be the one!"

A job seeker who "gets" both is far better equipped for the search and for the interview . . . and more likely to land the job.

In a tough job market, a hiring manager has plenty of good candidates to choose from. The person who shows flexibility and eagerness to learn has the advantage.

Adapt
Acclimate, accommodate, accustom, adjust, align, alter, change, comply, conform, fashion, fit, match, modify, prepare, readjust, revise, suit, tailor

Add
Annex, append, augment, bring, broaden, combine, complement, connect, contribute, enlarge, enrich, expand, fortify, heighten, increase, include, join, lend, supplement, total, unite, widen

Adept
Able, accomplished, capable, dexterous, effective, expert, experienced, good, polished, practiced, proficient, qualified, savvy, sharp, skilled, talented, versed

Administer
Administrate, apply, assign, conduct, control, direct, engineer, execute, govern, head, implement, lead, manage, officiate, operate, oversee, perform, preside, run, supervise

Advise
Caution, consult to, counsel, direct, guide, inform, instruct, notify, recommend, suggest, tutor

Advocate
Counsel, defend, promote, recommend, speak for, support, urge

Noun: counselor, champion

Allocate
Allot, apportion, appropriate, assign, budget, designate, distribute, grant, present, specify

Analyze
Break down, consider, determine, dissect, evaluate, examine, figure, inspect, investigate, judge, resolve, review, scrutinize, study

Quotes From The Queen

Although we include *assist* here, it's passive and weak, so we don't recommend its use. Instead, use *"Member of senior class team that planned and executed fund drive for. . . .,"* or *"Key contributor to group project who delivered necessary revisions by deadline."* It doesn't start with a verb, but it still does the job.

Apply
Address, assign, dedicate, devote, direct, employ, focus, practice, put in motion, use

Appraise
Analyze, approximate, assay, assess, calculate, estimate, evaluate, examine, gauge, measure, price, rate, size, study, survey, valuate

Approve
Affirm, agree, authorize, back, certify, clear, commend, confirm, endorse, license, pass, permit, praise, recommend, sanction, support, uphold, validate

Arrange
Adapt, array, construct, devise, distribute, draft, fix, format, group, order, organize, plan, position, prepare, schedule, sort

Assemble
Call together, collect, compile, configure, congregate, construct, convene, create, erect, fashion, form, join, make, mold, produce, set up, shape, summon

Assess
Apprise, compute, consider, determine, evaluate, gauge, judge, measure, rate, review, survey, valuate, weigh

Assist
Aid, help, support

Attend to
Accompany, add(ed), augment, be present at

Quotes From The Queen

Blogs in your job search: If you have a personal blog, and you're using your real name, be careful to not post what you don't want read by a potential employer. Prospective employers *will* Google your name more often than you can imagine, so be sure everything there represents you in a professional manner. See *Portfolio* on page 62 for a better way to use the Internet for your job search.

Blogs can be a wonderful way to increase your visibility by being a showcase for your skills and talents. However, it's time to leave behind (literally *delete*) the things of college and think ahead to your first real job. If you do keep a blog, make sure it is free of libel, slander, profanity, flames and personal attacks of any kind. Get rid of the Beer Pong tournament photos or anything else that might come back to haunt you. Save that stuff on your hard drive if it amuses you, but keep it out of the public domain. This advice also pertains to your public profiles on Facebook, MySpace, or any other social networking web site you may belong to. If your friends have tagged you in photos on their public pages, make sure you know what's out there. If you don't think it's appropriate, see what you can do to convince them to delete the pictures, or at the very least delete your name tag.

Editor's Note: URLs for all web sites mentioned in these pages can be found at the end of the book in the Resources section.

B

Budget
Verbs: Allocate, allot, allow for, apportion, calculate, estimate, forecast, plan, schedule

Build/built
To make: Assemble, construct, compile, engineer, establish, fabricate, fashion, form, manufacture, produce

Bolster or strengthen: Actualize, augment, boost, create, expand, heighten, improve, perfect

Buy
Acquire, finance, obtain, procure, purchase, requisition, subsidize

Quotes From The Queen

A business card for your job search? Of course, and call it a *contact card* if you're more comfortable with that term. It's an easy way for you to "leave word" with a network contact. Whether you're currently working for someone now or not, create a simple card *on good card stock.* You can do this on your computer, but only if you really know what you're doing, have a good printer, and use heavy card stock. Otherwise, use a local printer, an office store copy center, or one of the online services such as Vistaprint. List your name, phone number(s), e-mail address, web site/blog if you have one, a few key words or a tag line. Your street address and city aren't really needed. *(See page 78 for more about tag lines.)*

Note: This is not the place to get overly creative with fonts and colors unless you were a graphic design major and can highlight your talents in this way.

Chris Kendall
Writer and Editor

Business · Editorial · Technical

(555) 555-1212   c.kendall@gmail.com

---

*Chris Kendall is a generic pseudonym used throughout this book.

Yes, You Can Get That Job!

C

Careful
Accurate, attentive, cautious, conscientious, deliberate, detailed, diligent, meticulous, mindful, observant, precise, prudent, scrupulous, thorough, thoughtful, vigilant, watchful

Centralize(d)
Assemble, center, concentrate, consolidate, contain, converge, focus, gather, streamline

Champion
Advocate, build

Noun: advocate

Change
Adjust, alter, convert, correct, diversify, modify, reconstruct, refashion, remodel, transfer, transform, turn, vary

Check
Approve, analyze, ascertain, compare, confirm, examine, inquire, inspect, investigate, monitor, review, study, survey, verify

Clarify
Define, delineate, elucidate, explain, illuminate, illustrate, interpret, simplify

Coach
Direct, educate, guide, instruct, mentor, prepare, prompt, ready, school, train

Quotes From The Queen

Career Research Meetings: Richard Nelson Bolles, author of *What Color is Your Parachute?*, coined the term "informational interview" in the 1970s. However, this approach of talking with people at target companies is frequently abused: "I promise I won't ask for a job, but can I bring you my resume?" An informational interview also implies an interview that's given as a courtesy to someone who may or may not be qualified for the job. So, I don't recommend using the term. Instead, I prefer the term *Career Research Meeting*. It's simply a networking meeting.

This is a business conversation, preferably face-to-face, that addresses your field and career goals other than landing a job. Don't even bring your resume to a Career Research Meeting. Doing so changes the purpose of the meeting from research to job search. If you're asked for your resume, explain why you intentionally didn't bring it, and offer to send it by e-mail within 24 hours. Sending an electronic version of your resume makes it easy for them to forward to their network contacts. However, this is a great time to hand out your contact card.

Once you've reached a decision about your goal(s), request a second meeting, saying "You were helpful while I sorted things out. Now, I'm in full job-search mode and would appreciate your advice on my plans."

Take advantage of your "newness" in the real job market and land as many of these meetings as you can. You will learn as much about the real job market — if not more — than in any course you took in school. In today's competitive job market, career research meetings, and networking in general, will uncover those "hidden" jobs.

Collaborate
Combine, concur, conspire, cooperate, cooperate with, coproduce, interface, participate, work jointly, work together, work with

Collate
Arrange, assemble, collect, compare, gather, integrate

Compare
Analyze, assimilate, collate, consider, contemplate, contrast, differentiate, discriminate, distinguish between, equate, examine, inspect, liken to, liken, match, study, weigh

Compile
Accumulate, amass, arrange, assemble, catalog, collect, compose, consolidate, gather, make, organize

Complete
Accomplish, achieve, actualize, close, conclude, consummate, end, execute, finalize, finish, fulfill, perform, realize

Compose
Author, compile, comprise, conceived, consists of, constitute, construct, create, design, fashion, forge, formed, invent, originate, produce

Compute
Calculate, count, determine, estimate, figured, measure, reckon

Conceive
Conception, conceptualize, contrive, create, design, devise, discover, envision, form a conception of, formulate, imagine, originate, realize, think, visualize

Conduct
Administer, arrange, chair, control, command, direct, engineer, govern, guide, handle, head, lead, manage, operate, orchestrate, organize, oversee, pilot, run, steer, supervise

Quotes From The Queen

Contacts are the basis of your network. Make a list of contacts, starting with people you know well in school: friends, professors and their staff, college advisors, counselors, administrators, internship supervisors, campus job managers and coworkers, even if they're not students, etc. Then add friends from home, then your parents' friends, neighbors, old contacts from high school . . . everyone you can think of. In this tumultuous market, it pays to add to your list by attending business seminars in your new field. There you'll meet people with whom you can network . . . and you may even meet your new boss!

Think beyond the classroom. College campuses can be so insular that you can easily forget there's a world outside. Thinking beyond your immediate college environment will put your head in the right place for the job search, and for the real job market, where such expansive thinking is highly prized. When you're done with the first draft of your list, you'll be pleasantly surprised to see dozens or even hundreds of names.

Consolidate
Amalgamate, blend, centralize, coalesce, combine, compact, concentrate, integrate, join, meld, merge, streamline, strengthen, unify, unite

Construct
Build, create, design, devise, engineer, fabricate, formulate, manufacture, produce

Control
Administer, administrate, command, conduct, dictate, direct, dominate, govern, handle, instruct, lead, manage, operated, oversee, pilot, regulate, steer, supervise

Convert
Alter, change, metamorphose, modify, shift, transfigure, transform, translate, turn

Convey
Communicate, disclose, express, impart, pass on, project, put across, relate, transmit

Cooperate
Aid, assist, collaborate, coordinate, interface, participate, partner

Coordinate
Accommodate, adapt, adjust, align, arrange, attune, balance, combine, harmonize, integrate, organize, plan, proportion, reconcile, schedule, set up

Counsel
Verbs: Advise, advocate, consult, direct, encourage, guide, inform, instructed, recommend, prompt, suggest

Quotes From The Queen

Conduct (verb) is a good word, but can be too broad at times. *"Conducted training sessions for freshman work-study students,"* means what? Instead, say *"Led training sessions,"* if that's what you did, or *"Created training materials."* It gets to the point and it portrays what you really did more accurately.

Create
Author, build, cause, compose, conceive, contrive, design, develop, establish, fabricate, form, formulated, found, generate, initiate, institute, invent, make, organize, originate, plan, produce, set up, shape, start, visualize

Creative
Adept, artistic, imaginative, innovative, inspired, inventive, original, resourceful, skillful, talented

Cut
Abate, abbreviate, abridge, clip, condense, curtail, decrease, delete, eliminate, lessen, lower, pare, reduce, shorten, slash, trim, truncate

Quotes From The Queen

Cover letters are read and sought after by most employers because they display the candidate's ability to write, beyond the resume, which may have been written by someone else. They are frequently *the* body of an e-mail or, for on an online application, you may be provided a larger field in which to enter your letter. If you are submitting a resume on paper, however, your cover letter should be composed on matching paper, with a heading identical to your resume's heading. Cover letters can prove that you know how to write, a skill sought by employers.

Cover letters should be customized for *each* job for *each* employer. Every letter should make four key points, and no more:

1. Tell them where you saw the posting and that you're interested, and that your resume is attached.
2. Tell them why you want to work for *them.*
3. Match your relevant skills and talents to the requirements of the job.
4. Call for action (ask for the interview).

Do not turn your cover letter into a mini resume. Use it only to match yourself to the job. Its function is to persuade the reader to read your resume. ("Hey, she actually read the job description! Let me see her resume!")

D

Decide
Agree, conclude, determine, elect, establish, figure, judge, resolve, rule, select, settle, surmise, weigh

Delegate
Appoint, ascribe, assign, authorize, cast, charge, choose, commission, consign, depute, designate, elect, empower, license, mandate, name, relegate, select, transfer

Deliver
Administer, allot, bring, convey, dispense, distribute, give, impart, pass, provide, remit, supply, transfer, transmit, turn over

Demonstrate
Delineate, describe, display, exhibit, explain, evince, illustrate, present, prove, show

Design
Verbs: Arrange, blueprint, conceive, conceptualize, construct, contrive, create, delineate, develop, devise, draft, fabricate, fashion, form, formulate, frame, intend, invent, originate, plan, produce, propose

Determine(d)
Verbs: Ascertain, conclude, decide, establish, figure, judge, resolve, rule

Adjectives: Ambitious, decisive, driven, intent, persistent, resolute, serious

Quotes From The Queen

Descriptive words in your resume: Otherwise known as adjectives and adverbs, *carefully used*, these can bring life and color to your resume. I advocate the judicious use of them. If you overuse them by putting *"Successful. . . ,"* for example, in every bulleted item in your resume, it would soon lose all meaning. The best approach is to point out the successful result of your actions. For example, instead of saying *"Strong meeting management skills,"* say *"Reduced meeting time typically by 34%."*

Develop
Advance, create, cultivate, elaborate, enlarge, enrich, establish, expand, form, formulate, generate, heighten, improve, institute, mature, organize, originate, produce, promote

Devise
Arrange, blueprint, cast, chart, conceive, conceptualize, construct, contrive, craft, create, design, discover, draft, fabricate, fashion, form, formulate, imagine, invent, make, originate, plan, plot, prepare, shape

Diagnose
Analyze, canvas, determinate, distinguish, examine, finger, identify, interpret, investigate, pinpoint, study

Direct
Administer, advise, aim, command, conduct, control, counsel, define, govern, guide, head, influence, instruct, lead, manage, operate, order, oversee, pilot, regulate, rule, show, steer, supervise, teach

Disciplined
Adjectives: Accomplished, efficient, practiced, trained

Discover
Ascertain, detect, determine, discern, disclose, encounter, expose, find, identify, invent, learn, notice, observe, recognize, reveal, uncover, unearth, unmask

Distribute
Administer, allocate, allot, apportion, appropriate, assign, bestow, circulate, consign, dealt, disburse, dispense, disseminate, issue, parcel, sort, spread

Diversified
Assorted, different, disparate, divergent, miscellaneous, several, varied, various, wide-ranging

Quotes From The Queen

You may have noticed that the word *duties* isn't here. It's a word that says *"Things I had to do."* That's not the attitude you want to convey. Plus, it's merely descriptive, and not about the accomplishments and results you achieved. A job search is all about communicating your *accomplishments*.

In today's competitive job market, describing your achievements isn't an option. It's vital.

Divert
Alter, avert, change, deflect, detour, deviate, modify, rechannel, redirect, reorient, turn

Document
Verbs: Chronicle, enter, file, inscribe, record, register

Double
Amplify, augment, copy, duplicate, enlarge, grow, increase, magnify, multiply, pair, repeat, two-fold

Drive
Actuate, boost, compel, encourage, force, impel, induce, inspire, mobilize, move, press, prompt, propel, push, stimulate, thrust, urge

Duplicate
Copy, double, dualize, repeat, replicate, reproduce, second

Quotes From The Queen

What's your *elevator speech?* It's your 30-second (or 60-second or 2-minute) commercial. It's what you say in response to the question, *"What can you tell me about yourself?"* It's called an elevator speech — despite the fact that people seldom talk in elevators — because it's supposed to be short enough to say while on a brief elevator ride. It's really a *value statement* — it should address your value and what you bring to the job. It is not your work history, personal biography, or a list of courses you've taken.

Example:
I recently graduated with a degree in English that I'm excited to use, particularly in technical writing. I was on the editorial staff of our student magazine and wrote a few articles about software that some other students had developed.

Today's job market requires you to show how well you know yourself AND the value you bring to an employer.

E

Earn
Achieve, acquire, attain, collect, deserve, gain, merit, obtain, procure, rate, realize, reap, receive

Edit
Adapt, alter, amend, analyze, arrange, check, censor, collect, correct, draft, finish, modify, polish, prep, recalibrate, refine, revise, rewrite, select, style, tighten

Eliminate
Cancel, delete, disqualify, eradicate, exclude, liquidate, remove, suspend, waive

Encourage
Advocate, back, boost, embolden, fortify, galvanize, hearten, incite, impel, inspire, inspirit, promote, rally, sponsor, stimulate, stir, strengthen, support

Energetic
Active, driving, dynamic, enterprising, fresh, industrious, lively, spirited, tireless, vibrant, vigorous

Ensure
Ascertain, assure, certify, confirm, guarantee, make certain

Establish
Charter, constitute, create, effect, enact, endow, entrench, formulate, found, incorporate, install, institute, launch, organize, originate, place, plant, provide, sanction, start

Quotes From The Queen

E-mail address: for a job search, this should be somewhat professional. In other words, it shouldn't be cute or tacky or risqué. Use common sense.

chris.kendall@gmail.com is considerably better than hotchrisxxx@gmail.com. Use your college or alumni account if you will have it past graduation, or create a Gmail account.

Most employers today still prefer e-mail to texting, so use e-mail.

E-mail signature: You know this as the text that includes your name and other information at the end of an e-mail, inserted automatically by your e-mail program if you designate it as such. For job search purposes, it should contain your full name, your tag line, your phone number(s), your e-mail address and, if you have one, the URL of your web site or blog. Why your e-mail address, even though it's being *sent* by you at your e-mail address? So that the recipient can copy all your pertinent information from one spot into their electronic mail directory or address book.

Example:
  Chris Kendall
  Writer and Editor
  (555) 555-1212
  chris.kendall@gmail.com

Having a professional signature makes you easier to reach. Given your competition for jobs today, paying attention to details like this can only help you.

Estimate
Verbs: Appraise, approximate, assess, budget, calculate, compute, conclude, determine, evaluate, figure, forecast, gauge, guess, judge, measure, predict, rate, surmise

Evaluate
Appraise, ascertain, assay, assess, determine, estimate, examine, gauge, judge, measure, rank, rate, survey, weigh

Expand
Amplify, augment, balloon, bolster, broaden, develop, enlarge, extend, flourish, grow, increase, inflate, intensify, magnify, maximize, outspread, spread

Expedite
Accelerate, advance, aid, assist, boost, drive, enable, facilitate, forward, further, hasten, help, promote, quicken, rush, speed

Experience
Nouns: Background, education, knowledge, practice, skill, understanding

Experienced
Adjectives: Able, accomplished, capable, competent, expert, knowledgeable, masterful, practiced, proficient, qualified, rounded, seasoned, skillful, trained

Quotes From The Queen

Entry level: When describing yourself on your resume, or in your elevator speech or interview, don't use the phrase "entry level". Sure, employers know you're at the beginning of your career. But saying "I want an entry-level job" is pretty much the same as saying "I'll take anything." Suppose you have a talent or skill that can leapfrog you ahead of a very junior position, wouldn't you take it? Of course. Especially in today's volatile economy, it pays to be specific about the value you bring. Don't sell yourself short.

F

Facilitate
Advance, aid, assist, ease, expedite, further, help, promote, simplify, speed, support

Field
Area, avocation, bounds, discipline, domain, environment, expertise, occupation, realm, specialty, sphere, study, territory, vocation

Finalize
Complete, conclude, decide, end, finish, settle

Finance
Back, capitalize, endow, found, fund, promote, sponsor, subsidize, support, underwrite

Flexible
Adaptable, affable, amenable, compliant, cooperative, formative, manageable, open, receptive, resilient, responsive, versatile

Forecast
Verbs: Anticipate, augur, calculate, estimate, determine, figure, gauge, plan, predetermine, predict, project, reason, surmise

Quotes From The Queen

Your GPA: It's great that you worked hard for that high overall grade average. It represents one type of achievement. But employers, especially in a competitive job market, want more — they want to know what you can DO for them. So be sure to tell them about successes from your internships, campus jobs, volunteer work, and other activities.

What does the *greeting* on your voice mail sound like? Is it short? Friendly, yet professional? Useful? A job search is not the time to have a message recorded by a drunk friend, to use coarse language, or to display an attitude. Listen to your greeting with an employer's ear and re-do it if necessary.

If you are using your cell phone as your primary means of verbal contact, assign a separate ring tone to your friends and family, and another one that potential employers will use. This, along with a quick check of the caller ID, can tell you if you should answer the phone "Yo, wassup?" or "Good afternoon, this is Chris Kendall."

Formulate
Compose, contrive, create, design, develop, devise, draft, invent, originate, plan, prepare

Found
Begin, commence, create, erect, establish, form, initiate, institute, launch, organize, start

Furnish
Afford, endow, equip, outfit, provide, supply

Quotes From The Queen

Honesty on a resume and in presenting yourself throughout your job search is an absolute must. Not only is this the ethical way to present yourself, but once you're hired, your resume becomes a legal document. Lies or semi-truths in a resume can become very public grounds for getting fired, even years later, even if you had a 4.0 GPA, and even if you are a star performer on the job.

Regarding keywords, don't try "hidden text" (white text on a white background) or other tricks, because today's resume screening software will pick it up. Such methods tell an employer you are not being honest with them, AND that you're being lazy, so they will reject your resume. Instead, make sure your keywords are threaded throughout your resume.

G

Gain
Verbs: Accomplish, achieve, acquire, add, advance, attain, augment, benefit, earn, increase, obtain, procure, reach, realize, reap

Generate
Create, develop, devise, effect, fabricate, form, initiate, institute, introduce, make, originate, produce, yield

Guide
Verbs: Advise, channel, conduct, control, counsel, direct, educate, handle, head, instruct, lead, manage, navigate, oversee, point, show, steer, supervise, usher

Quotes From The Queen

Informational interview: This is what's commonly known as the name for the meeting you get with someone in your network in order to learn more about a company or possible job opening. I call them *career research meetings* instead, so see **Career Research Meetings** on page 18. It's the best way to tap the "hidden" (really, unadvertised) job market. Since only about 20-30% of available jobs are advertised, this is a great technique for discovering unlisted openings. On the surface, it may seem time-consuming to land a job using this strategy, but you'll be accessing a much larger range of opportunities. Networking is crucial for you at all times, but is especially so in today's job market.

H

Handle
Administer, command, conduct, control, deal, direct, execute, guide, head, manage, maneuver, operate, oversee, run, supervise, transact

Head
Administer, captain, command, control, direct, govern, guide, lead, manage, oversee, regulate, run, steer, supervise

Help
Advance, aid, assist, benefit, boost, contribute, cooperate, encourage, enhance, facilitate, further, improve, promote, support

Quotes From The Queen

Key words: Think of your resume not only as a marketing document, but as a miniature database of key words. At large organizations, your resume is entered into their resume bank for that opening or a future one. The hiring manager, or someone in the Human Resources department, has already created a list of key words for a particular job, and they look for resumes that make the best match. Those are the resumes that finally get looked at by human eyes.

Carry over the same key words on any of your public MySpace, Facebook, LinkedIn or Squidoo pages, web sites, or blogs so that you can be found by employers using searches of all kinds.

I

Identify
Analyze, certify, classify, determine, diagnose, discern, discover, distinguish, establish, found, label, name, pinpoint, select

Imaginative
Artistic, clever, constructive, creative, enterprising, ingenious, inspired, inventive, originative, resourceful

Implement
Actualize, apply, bring about, carry out, effect, employ, enable, execute, invoke, perform, start

Improve
Advance, ameliorate, augment, better, boost, develop, elevate, embellish, enhance, enrich, increase, lift, perfect, polish, refine, renew, revive, sharpen, strengthen, update, upgrade

Improvise
Brainstorm, compose, concoct, contrive, devise, extemporize, fabricate, invent

Increase
Verbs: Accrue, accumulate, advance, aggrandize, amplify, augment, boost, broaden, build, climb, compound, deepen, develop, elevate, enhance, enlarge, expand, extend, further, gain, grow, heighten, intensify, magnify, mount, multiply, raise, sharpen, strengthen, supplement, widen

Quotes From The Queen

More about *key words*: Generate a list of key words and phrases that you can swap in and out of your resume. Suppose you had a double major in software engineering and marketing (it could happen), and are qualified to work in both fields. A handy tool for you to have would be one list of key words that will work for software engineering positions, and another list for marketing. That way you have a *key word bank* to access when a job opens up unexpectedly, saving yourself a lot of effort and time customizing your resume and cover letter.

Influence
Nouns: Authority, character, clout, command, credit, jurisdiction, importance, inspiration, leadership, power, predominance, prominence, reputation, strength, weight

Verbs: affect, alter, change, control, convert, effect, guide, impel, impress, lead, persuade, sway

Initiate
Begin, cause, commence, establish, install, institute, introduce, facilitate, launch, open, organize, originate, pioneer, propose, start

Innovate
Change, introduce, modify, pioneer, reform

Inspect
Appraise, assess, audit, check, evaluate, examine, investigate, observe, probe, question, review, scan, scrutinize, search, study, survey

Inspire
Affect, drive, embolden, guide, impel, influence, motivate, spur, urge

Install
Establish, furnish, initiate, institute, introduce, place, plant, set up

Institute
Begin, commence, create, develop, enact, establish, form, found, initiate, introduce, launch, open, pioneer, start

Instruct
Acquaint, advise, brief, coach, command, counsel, direct, educate, guide, inform, lead, lecture, mentor, order, prepare, school teach, train

Instrumental
Key, important, vital, critical

Quotes From The Queen

Interviewing: Despite the countless books and other resources about interviewing and interviewing questions, there really are only five interview questions. Every interview question is one of these, whether the person asking it knows it or not:

- **Who are you?** Questions in this group include "Tell me about yourself."
- **Can you do the job?** Questions in this group include "Tell us about a time when you. . . ." and "Give me an example of when you. . . ."
- **Do you want to do the job?** These questions include "What motivates you to want to do this work?" and "Why do you want to work for us?"
- **Is there anything wrong with you?** Questions here include "Why did you leave that campus job?" and "How long have you been looking for a job?"
- **How much will you cost us?** Sample questions are "What salary are you looking for?" and "Can you describe your work habits?"

So when you hear an interview question, you can do a quick translation in your head to one of those five questions and you'll be able to answer it more easily.

Remember, interviewing doesn't stop when you land the job. Suppose a senior manager wants to know if you'll fit in on a certain project. Yes, she'll interview you. So be sure to focus on the *value* that you bring. That's why they'll hire you!

Integrate
Accommodate, amalgamate, assimilate, attune, blend, combine, compact, consolidate, coordinate, fuse, harmonize, incorporate, intersperse, join, link, merge, mingle, mix, unite

Interpret
Clarify, construe, define, delineate, describe, explain, illustrate, translate, understand

Interview
Nouns: Conference, consultation, meeting

Verbs: Confer, consult, converse, evaluate, probe, question

Introduce
Make known: Acquaint, announce, inform, present, propose

To begin: Commence, enter, establish, found, inaugurate, induct, initiate, insert, install, institute, interpolate, launch, present, submit

Invent
Author, compose, conceive, construct, contrive, create, design, devise, discover, fashion, forge, formulate, found, originate, patent, produce

Investigate
Analyze, check, examine, explore, inspect, inquire, probe, research, review, search, study

Quotes From The Queen

Layoffs: Don't let layoffs at your target companies scare you away. "Company A" may be letting people go in one area while hiring in others. So keep up the networking (see "Networking your way into a company," p. 50).

Language: Be careful with your language throughout your search. In other words, be sure to use the language used in your field today, and drop "like," "whatever" and other *fillers*. You want the focus on *what you can do*, not on your age, and not on your GPA.

How do you learn this "language?" By becoming familiar with publications and web sites in your prospective field, and by mixing with people in that field (networking). It's part of being a professional and it's essential in a competitive job market.

J

Judgment
Reasoning, decision-making, understanding, wisdom, rationale, logic, intuition, sense, good sense, prudence

Judicious
Accountable, astute, careful, diplomatic, discerning, discriminating, measured, prudent, rational, reasonable, responsible, thoughtful, trustworthy, wise

Juggle
Multi-task, balance, manage, organize, deal with, fit in

Quotes From The Queen

Motivation during the job search is critical to your success. One of my favorite things to say to job seekers is "There are no cat skeletons in trees." This is usually met with rolled eyes, so go ahead and roll.

But... have you ever *seen* a cat skeleton in a tree? There are no cat skeletons in trees because eventually they *do* come down. In the same way, you *will* get a job. So have faith that even if it takes longer than you'd like, you *will* get a job. Sometimes moments of faith like this, whether from these statements or your own, can fan the flames of motivation.

There's nothing mysterious about *networking:* it's just talking to and listening to people you know and people they know. If you "ask around" about the best personal trainer in town or a good hair stylist, and you get information that way, that's networking. It's the same when it comes to your career. Talk to people you know, listen to their ideas and the information they offer you, and you will expand your network.

It's been said that we each have 250 people in our active network. When you attend a career fair or networking meeting, especially one related to job search, someone in the room may very well know the hiring manager in a target company of yours. Asking for and providing information is the heart of networking.

K

Key
Basic, central, chief, crucial, critical, essential, fundamental, instrumental, important, leading, main, major, pivotal primary, principal, significant, vital

Knowledge
Ability, aptitude, awareness, comprehension, expertise, familiarity, grasp, mind, practice

Quotes From The Queen

Network your way into a company: See your school's alumni directory to learn if one or more grads are working at your target company. If so, connect with them and learn more about the company from the inside. This person will give you tips about how to be more competitive in your search within that company.

Networking Profile: This is a one-page synopsis of your accomplishments, skills, and talents for *networking* purposes. It is meant to be read by your networking contacts, not by employers. The goal of a networking profile is to provide enough information about you so that your networking contact can help and/or refer you on to other people who can help.

State your contact information and include a *Summary* like the one on your resume (it may even be identical). Because networking profiles are more broad-brushed than resumes with their detailed bullets, here you should include statements about your skills, your competencies, and your successes. List the places where you've worked, along with your titles, and end it with a list of target companies. Consider this a useful tool to use in a good or bad economy.

See **Professional Summary** on page 66 for more information about that part of a resume. See **Target Companies** on page 80 for more about that aspect of the job search.

L

Launch
Begin, commence, establish, found, initiate, institute, introduce, open, propel, start

Lead
Guide: Captain, conduct, drive, escort, handle, head, manage, pilot, regulate, steer, supervise

Influence: Advise, cause, direct, govern, persuade, spearhead, supervise

Learn(ed)
Verbs: Acquire, ascertain, attain, determine, discover, master, unearth

Adjectives: Academic, accomplished, experienced, knowledgeable, practiced, proficient, skilled, versed

Lower
Abate, curtail, decrease, deflate, diminish, downsize, drop, minimize, reduce, shave, slash

Quotes From The Queen

Networking web sites such as LinkedIn and Jobster, which now has a Facebook app that lets you convert your Facebook profile into a Jobster resume, are increasingly more influential within corporate talent acquisition (Human Resources) departments, and with hiring managers. Their reasoning: why not search a narrow database of potential candidates, rather than post an opening that will only bring us hundreds of non-qualified applicants? Enter a general profile on these sites and use them to expand your network. That's especially important in a weak economy.

M

Maintain
Continue, control, manage, perpetuate, preserve, proceed, retain, support, sustain, uphold

Manage
Administer, command, conduct, control, counsel, direct, engineer, govern, guide, handle, head, instruct, lead, maintain, officiate, operate, oversee, preside, regulate, steer, supervise

Market
Advertise, deal, dispense, exchange, furnish, merchandise, offer, package, retail, sell, trade, vend

Mathematical
Analytical, exact, precise, scientific, technical

Mediate
Arbitrate, broker, intercede, moderate, negotiate, reconcile, resolve

Merge
Amalgamate, assimilate, blend, centralize, combine, concentrate, consolidate, converge, fuse, incorporate, integrate, intermingle, join, meld, mingle, mix, unify, unite

Modernize
Better, develop, improve, redesign, redevelop, refresh, regenerate, rejuvenate, remake, remodel, renew, renovate, revamp, revive, update

Yes, You Can Get That Job!

Quotes From The Queen

Numerals: Just about every writing guide out there says the writer must spell out a number under 10 (zero, one, two . . .), and may use the numeral itself for numbers 10 or over. I usually break that rule because the appearance of a numeral on a resume (0, 1, 2 . . .) is more eye-catching (to both humans and screening software) than the number spelled out. So as you work on your resume, you can break this rule, too! It's my belief that a resume need not follow some approved rigid format, but instead it should be informative and readable.

Modify
Adapt, adjust, alter, change, convert, correct, edit, innovate, recast, refashion, reform, reorganize, reshape, revise, rework, shift, temper, transform, vary

Monitor
Audit, check, follow, observe, oversee, supervise, track, watch

Motivate
Activate, cause, drive, excite, fire, galvanize, impel, incline, induce, inspire, inspirit, move, persuade, pique, prompt, propel, rouse, spark, spur, stimulate

Multilingual
Linguist, polyglot

Multi-task
Juggle, balance

Quotes From The Queen

Online job search: Compare today's job search with one done by your parents or older friends or siblings, and you'll see a vast difference. The Internet has revolutionized the search. For example, today many companies won't look at faxed or snail-mailed resumes, only those that are e-mailed or submitted directly from their web site.

A word of caution: attempting to do a job search at your keyboard, without actually going to meetings or networking groups, will just about guarantee you a long, frustrating job search, or a job that you didn't really want but that "was available." You do want the best job you can get, right?

You can get sucked into *Craigslist* for hours everyday and eventually end up with a part-time position taking tickets in front of a club, or you can put yourself "out there" and pick up the phone.

N

Negotiate
Accommodate, adjust, agree, arbitrate, arrange, bargain, compose, compromise, concert, confer, contract, deal, debate, discuss, intermediate, mediate, settle, transact

Network
Verbs: communicate, connect, interact, find connections, establish connections, talk with others, exchange information

Nouns: contacts, connections, peers, associations, system of connections, people one knows

Notable
Outstanding, high profile, important, noteworthy, rare, well-known, serious, unique

Numerous
Plentiful, many

Quotes From The Queen

You don't see *oversee* or *oversaw* in this book, because *manage* and *direct* are better and more to the point about what you did. *Oversaw* is weak and means "watch over." It does not pass the "So what? Test" *(see page 76)* on your resume. If you *supervised* or *managed* something, then those are the words to use.

O

Observe

Obey: Adhere, comply, conform, follow, honor

Watch: Detect, discern, discover, follow, monitor, note, notice, perceive, saw, study, survey, view

Obtain
Access, accomplish, achieve, acquire, attain, collect, earn, gain, gather, get, procure, reach, realize, reap, secure, take

Open
Begin, commence, exhibit, expand, initiate, launch, spread, start, unbar, unfold

Operate
Administer, conduct, control, direct, drive, effectuate, engineer, function, handle, head, lead, manage, maneuver, perform, run, steer, work

Opportunity
Chance, moment, occasion, possibility, potential

Organize

Found: Build, construct, create, design, establish, fashion, form, institute, mastermind, mobilize, plan, shape, start

Order: Arrange, catalog, classify, coordinate, group, methodize, rank, regulate, structure, systemize, tailor

Quotes From The Queen

PDFs are valuable tools in the business world because they can be accessed by all computers, aren't easy to change, and because the file size can be reduced, which makes them easier to send over the Internet. But *DO NOT* use them in your job search, especially for your resume, unless you are specifically asked to do so! This is because most companies' screening methods are set up for Microsoft® Word only, and because recruiters will want to take your resume and make changes to it that fit their style. Sending a PDF without being asked for it is likely to mean your resume won't even get entered into a company's database, much less looked at by anyone there. In today's stiff job market, you sure don't need snags like that.

Portfolios are not just for art majors. In many cases, having a portfolio, whether in hard copy in a nice binder that you bring with you to interviews, or online, can help you in your job search. It's a collection of some of your best work, excellent reviews, letters of thanks, faculty advisor references, and so forth. This supports what you say in your resume with real-life examples. Costs can range from less than $20 for a paper version to $2,000 or more for the online type, which can get unnecessarily elaborate (with audio and video files) unless you're looking for a job in the entertainment industry. If you know how to create a web site, you can easily create a simple online version yourself.

Originate
Begin, compose, conceive, create, derive, design, develop, discover, draft, evolve, fashion, form, found, generate, initiate, innovate, institute, introduce, invent, launch, pioneer, produce, start

Overhaul
Audit, check, debug, fix, improve, inspect, mend, rebuild, recondition, reexamine, regenerate, reconstruct, renew, repair, restore, revamp, survey

Quotes From The Queen

Professional: The dictionary says this word means "one engaged in a profession, a skilled occupation based on education or training." But the word goes much further:

- A professional adheres to the standards and ethics of the profession
- A professional exhibits mature behavior: they are conscientious, courteous, business-like, ethical, and willing to do what it takes
- A professional achieves proficiency in the profession
- A professional applies knowledge in a way that benefits others.

Presenting yourself as a *professional* is part of the attitude that employers want to see in a candidate. In this competitive job market, displaying this quality will put you ahead of the fellow grad who does not let go of the "What's in it for me?" attitude.

P

Perform
Accomplish, achieve, complete, effect, execute, finish, fulfill, function, meet, operate, realize

Persuade
Affect, assure, cajole, coax, convert, convince, counsel, exhort, induce, influence, lead, prompt, reason, sway, urge

Plan
Verbs: Arrange, blueprint, calculate, cast, chart, craft, design, develop, devise, engineer, fabricate, form, formulate, frame, map, organize, outline, plot, prepare, project, schedule, shape, strategize

Prepare
Arrange, assemble, condition, develop, equip, fix, formulate, make, plan, qualify, ready

Present
Acquaint, cite, demonstrate, display, exhibit, give, introduce, manifest, offer, pitch, proffer, show, submit

Prioritize
Arrange, grade, order, place, rank, rate, schedule

Process
Verbs: Administer, analyze, handle, manage, prepare, treat

Quotes From The Queen

Professional Summary: This is the part of the resume right under your title, near the top of the first page. It describes you as a professional, regardless of your field or the fact that you're just beginning your career.

Here are a couple examples:

Customer-focused Technical Specialist with business operations knowledge. Intuitive problem solver skilled in managing complex projects. Energetic, with a track record of dependability.

Customer Service professional with strong sense of classic style. Friendly, diplomatic, energetic, organized, and efficient. Goal-oriented and self-motivated. Multi-tasks well; graceful under pressure. Readily assesses client's needs. Strong awareness of current trends. Management potential.

I recommend using such a summary because it tells a potential employer who you are. After all, people hire *people*, not resumes.

Be prepared to back up your claims by citing examples of your achievements in the bullet points under each job, internship, or volunteer activity. Today, employers want to see evidence, not promises.

Produce
Assemble, build, compose, construct, create, deliver, design, develop, fabricate, form, generate, invent, manufacture, originate, yield

Program
Verbs: Arrange, book, calculate, compute, control, design, figure, organize, plan, process, schedule, slate

Promote
Advance, aid, ascent, assist, back, better, bolster, boost, champion, elevate, encourage, endorse, forward, foster, further, graduate, help, hype, improve, launch, publicize, push, raise, recommend, sponsor, support, urge, upgrade

Propose
Advocate, assert, broach, introduce, offer, pose, present, proffer, recommend, solicit, suggest, submit, tender

Provide
Afford, bestow, endow, equip, fit, furnish, grant, outfit, supply, support

Purchase
Acquire, acquisition, attain, buy, earn, gain, get, invest, obtain, procure, realize, select

Quotes From The Queen

References available upon request is not needed on a resume. It just takes up valuable space you can use for something else that better sells you. It's *assumed* that you have references an employer can contact.

Your references are *not* part of your resume. Instead, they belong as a separate document. Have three or four, and these should be a mix: a former or current employer, a trusted faculty member who knows your work, an internship supervisor. Your professors will be useful as references for your first job post-graduation. After that, however, use managers and others who know your most recent work. These will carry far more weight as time goes on.

You should have their name, phone number, and e-mail address for ease of contact, though they will most likely receive a phone call. Also vital: a brief phrase that describes who they are to you. *"Professor of _____ at _____University,"* is plenty.

It is important to treat your references like gold. Stay in touch with them throughout your search, thank them often, and let them know what happens. If they are instrumental in your finding that great job, a personal letter or phone call would be greatly appreciated.

Q

Qualified
Adjectives: Able, accomplished, adept, capable, certified, competent, disciplined, efficient, eligible, equipped, experienced, expert, instructed, knowledgeable, licensed, practiced, proficient, proved, skilled, skillful, suitable, suited, tested, trained, versed

Quality
Ability, aspect, attribute, element, factor, features, traits

Quotes From The Queen

Coach your *references!* They will appreciate your reminding them of the various projects you did or that you worked on together, and what you did to make the project successful. Ensure that each of them says something substantial about you AND says something *different* than the other references will say about you. It's nice if all of them say you're a hard worker, but not as effective as if each says something important about you. So one reference may emphasize your ability to lead teams, while another may focus instead on how well you use limited resources. Another may be able to address your strengths *and* your main weakness, neutralizing the latter so that you don't have to. Doing this describes you in a more well-rounded way to a prospective employer.

R

Raise
Verbs: Advance, amplify, augment, boost, elevate, grow, heighten, hike, increase, inflate, lift, promote, rise, uplift

Receive
Accept, acquire, admit, assume, collect, gain, get, incur, inherit, obtain, redeem, secure, take

Recommend
Acclaim, advise, advocate, applaud, approve, celebrate, commend, endorse, praise, prize, propose, sanction, suggest, support, urge

Record
Catalog, chronicle, document, enter, enumerate, file, indicate, list, log, maintain, mark, note, register, report, tabulate, written

Recruit
Engage, enlist, enroll, enter, gather, get, induct, obtain, procure, select

Redesign
Change, engineer, improve, refresh, regenerate, revise, revive

Reduce
Abate, abbreviate, abridge, clip, condense, consolidate, curtail, cut, decrease, dilute, diminish, downgrade, lessen, limit, lower, minimize, pare, restrict, shave, shorten, slash, taper, trim

Quotes From The Queen

"Responsible for...." **Do not use this phrase!** That's why you don't see it here. It's a phrase that's passive and it doesn't highlight your *accomplishments*. If you *managed*, or *organized*, or *coordinated* something, say so. If you were asked to do something, talk about how you were *selected* to do this, *recruited* to do it.

Refine
Better, clarify, enhance, hone, improve, perfect, polish, smooth

Relate(d)
Verbs: Chronicle, describe, narrate, recount, report, state, tell

Adjectives: Affiliate, ally, associate, cognate, complementary, concern, connect, correlative, correspond, interconnect, kindred, link, pertain, pertinent, relevant

Reliable
Conscientious, devoted, established, honest, positive, proved, reputable, respectable, responsible, sincere, solid, sound stable, steady, trustworthy

Reorganize
Change, improve, readjust, rearrange, reconstruct, regroup, reorder, revise

Repair
Correct, fix, mend, overhaul, rebuild, recondition, rectify, refurbish, remedy, renovate, restore, revamp, service

Report
Account, announce, broadcast, communicate, declare, describe, disclose, document, inform, note, notify, present, publish, record, relate, state

Represent
Act for, delineate, denote, depict, epitomize, exemplify, personify, picture, portray, serve, steward, symbolize, typify

Research
Verbs: Analyze, delve, examine, explore, investigate, probe, search, scrutinize, study

Nouns: Analysis, assessment, examination, inquiry, review

Quotes From The Queen

What is a resume's function? Your resume's function is to get you *the interview*. It's not an accounting of every single job you've had since you were 14, or every course you've taken since Freshman Year. A resume is a marketing document that should be designed to convince someone that you will be worth talking to. That means it should focus on what you bring to the job, what makes you interesting, and what's relevant to your career goals, both short- and long-term.

Resolve
Verbs: Analyze, answer, clear, conclude, decide, determine, decipher, discern, dispel, establish, figure, fix, settle, unravel

Nouns: Character, drive

Responsibility
Accountability, authority, capabilities, care, charge, commitments, contract, duty, jurisdiction, liability, obligation, requirement

Responsible
Accountable, capable, competent, conscientious, creditable, effective, efficient, judicious, qualified, sensible, stable, sound, steady, trustworthy

Restore
Improve, rebuild, reconstruct, recover, reestablish, regain, reinstate, rejuvenate, renew, repair, replace, return, revive

Retrieve
Recapture, reclaim, recoup, recuperate, recover, regain

Review
Verbs: Analyze, assess, check, critique, edit, evaluate, examine, inspect, interpret, judge, reconsider, reevaluate, scrutinize, study, survey, weigh

Revise
Alter, amend, change, correct, edit, improve, modify, perfect, polish, redraft, reorganize, restyle, retool, revamp, rework, rewrite, tighten, update, upgrade

Quotes From The Queen

The "So What?" test: Does every bullet on your resume pass the *"So What?"* test? In other words, does it address some aspect of your value to an employer? Or does it just make a statement to which we can say *"Well, so what?"* Avoiding the *"So What?"* syndrome on your resume will set you above and beyond your competition in today's job market. For more on this, see ***Value*** on page 88.

S

Schedule
Arrange, book, engineer, organize, plan, plot, record, register, slate

Select
Choose, cull, decide, determine, elect, name, opt, pick, prefer

Sell
Auction, close, deal, give, liquidate, market, merchandise, retail, supply, trade, vend, wholesale

Serve
Act, aid, assist, attend, foster, fulfill, function, handle, help, officiate, promote, work

Service
Aid, assist, help, maintain, sustain

Set up
Arrange, assemble, began, construct, create, erect, establish, found, inaugurate, institute, open, prearrange, prepare, start

Show
Convince, demonstrate, direct, display, exhibit, explain, guide, illustrate, inform, instruct, lead, note, present, reveal, tell

Simplify
Abridge, clarify, clear, condense, explain, interpret, minimize, shorten, streamline

Yes, You Can Get That Job!

Quotes From The Queen

Tag lines are simply short, catchy statements about who you are and what you do. They make it easier to explain your value when you're talking with a potential employer or when you're networking.

One of my clients, Mike, dubbed himself *"The Geek Who Can Speak"* because as technical as he was, he was also good at marketing and sales — not a common combination of skills. For anyone who meets him and who cannot remember his name, as soon as you say, "You know him; he's the Geek Who Can Speak," sure enough the other person says, "Oh yeah, I know who you mean."

Adding the tag line to your resume is another method that helps set you apart, in a good way, from the other resumes in the pile.

Solve
Answer, calculate, clarify, decipher, decode, determine, elucidate, explain, figure, fix, reason, resolve, settle, unfold, unlock, unravel, untangle, work

Sort
Arrange, catalogue, categorize, class, classify, file, grade, group, index, list, order, rank, screen, type

Spark
Activate, excite, incite, initiate, inspire, kindle, start, stimulate, trigger

Spearhead
Begin, chair, command, direct, head, lead, marshal, mastermind, organize, pioneer, start, steer

Staff
Verbs: Employ, supply

Standardize
Assimilate, institutionalize, normalize, order, regiment, regulate, systemize

Start
Activate, begin, commence, create, embark, establish, found, implement, inaugurate, initiate, institute, introduce, issue, launch, lead, open, organize, originate, pioneer

Streamline
Abridge, align, centralize, compact, concentrate, consolidate, contour, organize, reduce, simplify

Quotes From The Queen

Target companies: These are the companies or organizations where you think you'd love to work. Develop this list by doing research and matching your values and goals with what you learn about particular companies. Those that fit you end up on the list. Next step: networking your way into a select few of these companies.

Why is this better than just applying anywhere and everywhere? While it's good to get your resume into as many hands as possible, being focused increases the odds that your efforts will get you results. In today's competitive job market, knowing who you're going after helps you focus your research and your networking (see page 50). It also helps others help you — if you say you want Company A, your networking contacts may know someone there. Today, you need this kind of approach.

Strengthen
Add, bolster, brace, empower, energize enhance, fortify, heighten, increase, intensify, reinforce, secure, sharpen, stabilize, substantiate, support, tone, vitalize

Structured
Adjectives: Arranged, disciplined, formed, logical, methodized, methodical, ordered, organized, precise, systematic

Study(ied)
Verbs: Analyze, calculate, consider, contemplate, deliberate, examine, inspect, research, survey

Adjectives: Intentional, knowledgeable, purposeful, thoughtful, thought-out

Succeed
Accomplish, achieve, arrive, attain, earn, ensue, flourish, follow, fulfill, conclude, realize, reach, reach the goal

Success(ful)
Fortunate, lucrative, noteworthy, outstanding, productive, profitable, prosperous, rewarding, strong, thriving

Summarize
Abridge, condense, encapsulate, recap, restate, review, synopsize

Supersede
Countermand, follow, invalidate, override, overrule, overturn, replace, supplant, usurp

Supervise
Administer, advise, conduct, control, direct, guide, handle, head, manage, overlook, oversee, regulate, run, steer, superintend

Quotes From The Queen

Thank-you notes: An often forgotten or discounted courtesy, thank-you notes are an important part of the job search. With e-mail communication increasingly supplanting physical letters, a hand-written note has new meaning. A thank-you note to an interviewer or business contact is not only an appreciated gesture, it also shows that you are professional enough (and interested enough) to take the extra time to properly express your gratitude.

Thank-you notes also help to bolster your name recognition. Many positions go to the more persistent candidates for the simple reason that their names are fresh in the minds of the hirer. In addition to displaying your own politeness, you also get your name out there an additional time.

When writing a thank-you note, keep it short and to the point. There's no need to get sappy or to exaggerate. Your contact will appreciate a simple thank you and an expression of interest in the open position. You don't need to pledge the lives of your future children to the service of the company. Also, make sure you choose a fairly reserved looking note card rather than one loaded with flowery lettering and glitter.

If the note gets longer than a short sentence or two, then write a business letter or send an e-mail. For instance, if you want to give an interviewer one more example of how you led teams, a longer letter or e-mail will be preferable.

Supply
Afford, deliver, dispense, endow, equip, fulfill, furnished, give, grant, issue, outfit, provide, stock

Support
Verbs: Advocate, aid, approve, assist, back, bolster, champion, encourage, endorse, fund, promote, reinforce, shoulder, sponsor, sustain, uphold

Systematize
Arrange, design, devise, establish, frame, institute, methodize, order, organize, plan, regulated, standardize

Quotes From The Queen

Typecasting: Don't be put off by network contacts who aren't as familiar as you are with technology you take for granted (IM or texting on your cell, for example). There are many employers who are leaders in their fields, but who hardly ever turn on their cell phones. Understand there are many levels of expertise: you have some, employers have others, and you both need one another.

T

Tabulate
Arrange, catalogue, categorize, chart, classify, codify, count, formulate, index, inventory, list, order, record, register

Tailor
Accommodate, adapt, adjust, alter, conform, convert, fashion, modify, mold, shape, style, trim

Teach
Advise, coach, demonstrate, direct, educate, explain, guide, illustrate, inform, instruct, prepare, ready, school, train, tutor

Tend
Administer, attend, control, cultivate, direct, follow, foster, guard, handle, maintain, manage, mind, minister, oversee, supervise, watch

Terminate
Abort, cancel, cease, close, complete, conclude, culminate, discharge, discontinue, dismiss, dissolve, drop, eliminate, end, expire, finish, leave, resign, stop

Total
Verbs: Add, calculate, compute, count, figure, reckon, tally

Nouns: Amount, sum, tally

Trace
Follow, search, track, watch

Track
Chase, follow, hunt, observe, pursue, trace, trail

Yes, You Can Get That Job!

Quotes From The Queen

I could have added the affected *utilize* but, preferring the power of simplicity, I don't like the word because it uses three syllables when *use* uses one. Don't try to sound like a lawyer in a legal document. This is your resume, so use *use* instead.

Trade
Verbs: Bargain, barter, deal, exchange, negotiate, substitute, swap
Nouns: Art, avocation, business, craft, line, occupation, position, profession, skill, vocation

Train(ed)
Verbs: Coach, cultivate, develop, direct, educate, equip, guide, groom, hone, instruct, practice, prepare, prime, school, season, shape, taught, tutor
Adjectives: Accomplished, adept, competent, disciplined, educated, inform, proficient, qualified, schooled, skilled

Transfer
Assign, change, convey, delegate, dispatch, dispense, hand, move, reassign, relegate, relocate, remove, re-station, send, shift, transplant

Transform
Alter, change, convert, metamorphose, modify, mold, reconstruct, revamp, switch, vary

Translate
Construe, decipher, decode, elucidate, explain, interpret, paraphrase, transcribe, turn

Transport
Bring, carry, convey, fare, ferry, move, send, shift, ship, truck

Trim
Clip, crop, curtail, cut, decrease, lessen, minify, pare, reduce, shave, shorten, tailor, truncate

Triple
Increase, multiply, threefold, thrice, triad, trio

Quotes From The Queen

Value: This might be the most important page in this book, because your VALUE is what employers are looking for, especially today. Your value (V Factor) is measured in three ways. Not everyone can *score* in all three ways. It's great if you can, but some occupations lend themselves to one over the others.
These V Factors are:

1. Saving or making money. A successful salesperson makes money for a company; an accountant saves money.

2. Saving or making time. Now you really can't do either of those things with time, but you can create time for another person by, for example, picking up some work from someone else. An intern who takes on a task that frees up an engineer for several hours during a project is someone who's proving their value to everyone around them.

3. Solving problems. The person who says "I'll take care of that," and then does take care of it, becomes valuable to everyone around them.

During a job search, all your communications with a potential employer should address at least one of these. Your value is what gets you hired, not what you know or what your GPA is.

U

Uncover
Bare, disclose, discover, display, divulge, expose, impart, reveal, show, uncover, unearth, unmask, unveil

Undertake
Attempt, begin, commence, contract, endeavor, engage, initiate, launch, shoulder, start, try, venture, volunteer

Unify
Affiliate, ally, amalgamate, blend, combine, compound, concert, consolidate, harmonize, integrate, join, merge, mingle, mix, unite

Unravel
Decipher, disentangle, figure, separate, solve, unfold, undo, unscramble

Update
Bring up to date: Amend, modernize, modify, refresh, rejuvenate, renew, restore, revise

Impart knowledge: Advise, brief, counsel, explain, familiarize, inform, report

Use
Accept, adopt, apply, employ, exercise, operate, practice, utilize

Quotes From The Queen

Leave a *voice mail* that will get results. If you're following up after sending a resume, a good voice mail restates your value: *"Hi, this is Chris Kendall, the tech support specialist who reduces response time by 25%, calling to follow up on the resume I sent two weeks ago."* That kind of message gets a better response than *"I'm following up on the resume I sent,"* all by itself and helps you be more competitive today.

V

Vacate
Abandon, abdicate, abjure, clear, depart, discharge, empty, leave, relinquish

Various
Assorted, changing, different, distinctive, diverse, individual, multiple, numerous varied

Verify
Attest, authenticate, certify, check, confirm, establish, guarantee, prove, substantiate, test, validate

Quotes From The Queen

Welcome to the real world. Today's job search is vastly different than it was a generation ago. Ask your parents how they found their first jobs and you'll hear it firsthand. Early on in their careers, they'd walk into a company, ask to speak to someone or fill out an application. They may have been interviewed and hired on the spot.

It used to be that employees were rewarded for loyalty with the security of lifelong jobs. They worked their way up a career ladder. A job search was something you did once or twice after you completed your education, and then you could practically count on promotions to take you into retirement. Today, with corporate mergers and layoffs, outsourcing jobs overseas, and a host of other factors, your career path may be more like rock climbing: sometimes you go up, sometimes sideways, and sometimes you have to step down a bit before you find a place where you can settle down.

W

Weigh
Analyze, appraise, balance, consider, contemplate, deliberate, estimate, evaluate, examine, measure, ponder, reflect, study

Widen
Augment, broaden, enlarge, expand, extend, grow, increase, multiply, spread, stretch

Win
Achieve, acquire, attain, conquer, earn, gain, got, net, overcome, prevail, reach, realize, secure, succeed

Withdraw
Abjure, disengage, leave, recant, recede, remove, renounce, rescind, retire, retract, retreat

Withstand
Bear, brave, confront, endure, face, hold, oppose, resist, stand, take, tolerate, traverse

Work
Commission, conduct, employ, function, labor, operate, practice, perform, specialize, strive, travail

Write
Author, compose, correspond, create, draft, formulate, note, pen, pencil, publish, record, transcribe

Online Resources

www.careerbuilder.com

www.careerjournal.com

www.craigslist.org

www.federalgovernmentjobs.us

mail.google.com

www.guru.com

www.hotjobs.com

jobs.imdiversity.com

www.indeed.com

www.job-hunt.org

www.jobster.com

www.linkedin.com

www.monster.com

www.nyfa.org

www.simplyhired.com

www.snagajob.com

www.squidoo.com

www.theresumequeen.com

Index

A

Accomplishments 28, 52, 73
Attitude 10, 28, 64

B

Beer Pong 14
Blogs 14, 16, 32, 42
Bolles, Richard Nelson 18
Business cards 16. See also Contact cards

C

Caller ID 36
Career fair 50
Career Research Meetings 18, 40
Contact card 16, 18
Contacts 20
Cover letters 24, 44
Craigslist 58

D

Descriptive words 26

E

E-mail 16, 32, 82
E-mail signature 32
Elevator speech 30, 34

F

Facebook 14, 42, 54

G

Gmail 32
Google 14
GPA 10, 36, 48, 88

H

Honesty 38

I

IM 84
Informational interview 18, 40

J

Jobster 54

K

Key word bank 44
Key words 6, 16, 42, 44

L

Layoffs 48
Language 48
LinkedIn 42, 54

M

Motivation 50
MySpace 14, 42

N

Networking 40, 48, 50, 52, 58, 78, 80
Networking groups 58
Networking Profile 52. See also Professional Summary
Networking web sites 14, 54
Numerals 56

O

Online job search 58

P

PDF 62
Portfolios 62
Professional Summary 52, 66. See also Networking Profile

R

References 62, 68, 70
Resume 6, 18, 24, 38
    bullet points in 26
    function of 74
    numerals in 56
    online job search and 58
    PDFs and 62
    summary in 52, 66
    taglines and 78
Resume bank 42

S

"So What? Test" 60, 76
Squidoo 42

T

Tag lines 16, 78
Target companies 18, 48, 52, 80
Thank-you notes 82
Typecasting 84

V

Value 30, 46, 76, 88
Value statement 30
V Factors 88
Voice mail 36, 90

Acknowledgments

My thanks go to my editor, Julie Murkette, and the early readers whose careful research and suggestions gave depth to many sections of this book.

And to David Balzotti, who patiently urged me on while I was writing it.

About the Author

Joanne Meehl is a career transition management consultant and author of *The Resume Queen's Job Search Thesaurus and Career Guide for Professionals*.

In graduate school, Joanne had an internship in a college counseling center and then landed a job in a community college near Boston. The students' concerns were all about their careers. She loved the work and never looked back. Today she works with people of all ages who don't just want a job; they want a satisfying career.

Joanne is also a widely published writer whose work has appeared in *The Washington Post*, *The Boston Globe*, CareerBuilder.com, CNN.com, and Monster.com.